THIS BOOK BELONGS TO
The Library of

....

....

©COPYRIGHT 2024

The content contained within this book may not be reproduced, duplicated, or transmitted without direct written permission from the author or the publisher. Under no circumstances will any blame or legal responsibility be held against the publisher, or author, for any damages, reparation, or monetary loss due to the information contained within this book. Either directly or indirectly.

Legal Notice:
This book is copyright protected. This book is only for personal use. You cannot amend, distribute, sell, use, quote, or paraphrase any part, or the content within this book, without the consent of the author or publisher.

Disclaimer Notice:
Please note the information contained within this document is for educational and entertainment purposes only. All effort has been executed to present accurate, up-to-date, and reliable, complete information. No warranties of any kind are declared or implied. Readers acknowledge that the author is not engaging in the rendering of legal, financial, medical, or professional advice. The content within this book has been derived from various sources. Please consult a licensed professional before attempting any techniques outlined in this book. By reading this document, the reader agrees that under no circumstances is the author responsible for any losses, direct or indirect, which are incurred as a result of the use of the information contained within this document, including, but not limited to — errors, omissions, or inaccuracies.

Thank you for Purchasing my book and taking the time to read it from front to back. I am always grateful when a reader chooses my work and I hope you enjoyed it!

With the vast selection available online, I am touched that you chose to be purchasing my work and take valuable time out of your life to read it. My hope is that you feel you made the right decision.

I very much would like to know what you thought of the book. Please take the time to write an honest and informative review on Amazon.com. Your experience and opinions will be of great benefit to me and those readers looking to make an informed choice.

With much thanks.

Table of Contents

Part 1: How to Buy Land	8
Chapter 1 – The First Secret of Wealthy Real Estate Investors: Investing in Land Can Be Just as Lucrative as Buying and Selling Homes	9
Chapter 2 The Second Secret of Wealthy Real Estate Investors: Know When to Buy and When to Sell	15
Chapter 3 The Third Secret of Wealthy Real Estate Investors: Have a Plan	17
Chapter 4 The Fourth Secret of Wealthy Real Estate Investors: Know Your Finances and Buying Options	19
Chapter 5 The Fifth Secret of Wealthy Real Estate Investors: Understand the Purchase Process	25
Chapter 6 The Sixth Secret of Wealthy Real Estate Investors: Decide What Kind of Land is the Best for You to Buy	28
Chapter 7 The Seventh Secret of Wealthy Real Estate Investors: Finding Good Land Deals	33
Part 2: Doing Your "Due Diligence"	45
Chapter 8 The Eighth Secret of Wealthy Real Estate Investors: Avoid Poor Choices	46
Chapter 9 The Ninth Secret of Wealthy Real Estate Investors: Research is Everything!	49
Chapter 10 The Tenth Secret of Wealthy Real Estate Investors: Utilize the Experts	61
Part 3: What to Do with Raw Land	69
Chapter 11 The Eleventh Secret of Wealthy Real Estate Investors: Find Uses for Your Land	70
Chapter 12 The Twelfth Secret of Wealthy Real Estate Investors: Know How to Sell Your Land	79

Introduction

When I was growing in in Las Vegas my parents didn't have much money, but they picked up a piece of land in a desert area 30 miles outside of Vegas, not far off Boulder Highway. It took about 10 minutes to get to the land on dirt roads. Although they only paid around $3000 for it, I remember they made payments on it for years. Then they had to figure out a way to pay for assessments when the developer began to bring power and water to the property, but they managed it.

We occasionally took family outings to go see "our land." We'd drive out to the desert and find the dirt lot. My father would walk the lot, finding the markers and put rocks near them, so he could see them better. We would talk about how they would retire there and build their dream house. We watched as people began building nice custom homes on sporadic lots around us.

Then, about 15 years later some financial troubles hit my parents in the form of medical bills when my mother developed cancer. After much consideration, they sold the land. And received $36,000, an 1100% increase.

No, they never did build their dream house, and ended up staying in the modest home they purchased years before (also a good investment, but that's another story), but the property was there for them when they needed the money the most. It turned out to be a great investment and emergency savings plan for them.

I wonder sometimes what would have happened if they could have bought more land at the right time. I think this is one of the reasons why I am fascinated with land sales and property ownership. I've seen how it can benefit ordinary people as well as the wealthy.

There are so many reasons why land can be a good investment—but not only can there be great opportunities in land ownership, there can be risks and pitfalls as well. That's why I am writing this book. I want to give ordinary people the advantages and knowledge that the wealthy use to be sure that the investments they make in land and real estate are wise choices and better risks for increasing their profits.

The wealthy and mega-rich know how important it is to hold part, or even the majority, of their fortunes in real estate. U.S. millionaires see real estate investment as the top alternative-asset class to own, according to according to a survey released by Morgan Stanley in 2014.

About 77 percent of investors with at least $1 million in assets own real estate. Direct ownership of residential and commercial properties was the number one alternative-investment pick for 2014, with a third of millionaires surveyed saying they planned to buy real estate that year. Twenty-three percent said they expect to invest in real estate investment trusts, the second-most popular choice. 1(http://www.bloomberg.com/news/articles/2014-02-06/millionaires-see-real-estate-as-top-investment-for-2014)

Here's what some of them have said about real estate investing:

- Donald Trump — "It's tangible, it's solid, and it's beautiful. It's artistic from my standpoint and I just love real estate."
- Robert Kiyosaki— "Real estate investing, even on a very small scale, remains a tried and true means of building an individual's cash flow and wealth."
- Armstrong Williams— "Now, one thing I tell everyone is learn about real estate. Repeat after me: real estate provides the highest returns, the greatest values and the least risk."

Multitudes of people understand how buying houses can make them a fortune, or at least a good living, by renting them out or flipping homes. This is attested by the many real estate infomercials and television shows on this subject. But not many people understand that buying and selling land can bring the same results, and without as much effort as investing in homes or commercial properties. This is one of the secrets many wealthy real estate investors know.

Unfortunately, there can also be serious risks in land investment, just as there can be when investing in homes, or anything else for that matter. It is very important that you know what you are doing when you buy land, or you could lose much of your money. The goal of this book is to teach some basic principles that can put you ahead of the pack and give you a much better chance at making money on your land investments.

Please understand— all investments are risks. I cannot guarantee that you will make money with this or any other investment. I can't control the economy, government regulations, international banking and the stock market. I have no idea what the political and economic situation will be at the time you read this book. As I write it, we are coming close to an election that probably will seriously impact economic factors in the United States. Will it be favorable for real estate investment? I can hope and try to make educated guesses, but in reality I have no idea. On the other hand, I can teach you some basic techniques the wealthy have used for decades to help them survive and even thrive in even the worst of financial markets and situations. How you apply these principals will be up to you.

Part 1: How to Buy Land

Chapter 1 – The First Secret of Wealthy Real Estate Investors: Investing in Land Can Be Just as Lucrative as Buying and Selling Homes

Why should you buy land? You may be one of the millions of people considering the idea of investing in land, and now you want to make sure that you're making the right decision before you buy land. The wealthy know this secret investment tool can be powerful. While most real estate investors avoid land, the wealthy are quietly busy purchasing it— doing the opposite of what everyone else is doing.

During the worst of the 2008-10 real estate crises, when everyone was fleeing or trying to sell their real estate, real estate mogul Donald Trump was buying up, among other things, golf courses all over the country at discount prices.

Why golf courses? This was a very smart strategy. Not only are golf courses expensive land— landscaped and well taken care of, and usually connected to expensive homes, but golf courses can be used in other ways if need be. You could easily turn a golf course into a five star resort, or a very nice home development.

There could be other reasons for buying golf courses too. Back in 1992 Steve Wynn bought an older struggling resort in Las Vegas called the Dunes, for a great sale price— only $75 million (it was bought by a previous owner, Japanese investor Masao Nangaku, in 1987 for $155 million.) Steve Wynn ended up blowing up parts of the Dunes casino for a piece of spectacular publicity and building the Bellagio in its place. Yes, the land the Dunes sat on was prime Las Vegas Strip real estate, but there were other pieces of land on the Strip available at that time that Steve could have purchased.

One of the biggest jackpots that Steve Wynn received with the purchase of the older resort was the historic Dunes golf course. It just happened that this golf course had an old well on it. In Las Vegas, a growing desert city in the middle of a drought, with a slowly sinking water table, there are strict water regulations imposed. But the well on the Dune's golf course came with grandfathered water rights, which pre-dated the new water regulations. With this well, anyone who owned the property had totally unrestricted water rights. Steve Wynn had plans for huge lavish fountains at the Bellagio, and with this well on the Dunes golf course, he could do whatever he wanted.

If you ever wondered how Las Vegas could allow resorts like the Mirage or the Bellagio to run their world famous fountains 24/7, when the rest of the city was under severe water restrictions, now you know the reason.

Plus, the land where the old Dunes golf course was once located is now occupied by parts of the Monte Carlo, the New York-New York, the CityCenter, the now-demolished Boardwalk Hotel and Casino, and the Cosmopolitan. Forget the resort and the expensive land the Dunes sat on, the old Dunes golf course turned out to be an amazingly smart purchase for Steve Wynn. (We won't get into the ethics of unrestricted water usage in a desert city... That's for another book.)

Now, of course, if you are like me, you can't go out and buy a Las Vegas golf course (by the way, at the time of this writing, I know of a good one for sale right now— with water rights, too) but we can use some of the same strategies and principals the wealthy use on a smaller scale.

Here are some of the reasons why wealthy real estate investors make the jump into land investment:

You Don't Have to Do Much With Land

When you own land, there is no home maintenance or dealing with problem renters. You don't have to rehab anything. Land is pretty much problem-free. Land is a long-term asset that doesn't wear out, doesn't depreciate like a manufactured home, and there is not much that can get broken, stolen or destroyed.

Land is a Stable Investment

There may be some fluctuations depending on the economy and other factors, but when held over the long term, land is a very stable investment in comparison to other investment types. It is usually considered a conservative investment, but depending on the area and the market, it can have amazing exponential growth.

Land is a Tangible Investment

While banks are experiencing credit problems and paper money value is at serious risk, with land you have your physical investment intact. If anything, it's always great to have an asset that you can actually see, touch, visit and walk on. The security you get from a physical investment is simply incomparable. No matter what the economy does, you have a piece of land you can still use for something. (See Chapter 11 for some good ideas on how to use your land.)

Land has Greater Long-Term Returns

There is a limited amount of land available in the world. With the heavy investment in land currently rising from the unstable financial markets, you can expect a shortage in this valuable asset in the future, which means that the value of land will appreciate. As the banking sector weakens, investing in property becomes a wiser option.

Investing in Land is Lower Risk

Historically, the value of land has always had an upward trend. There is only a finite amount of land and it is only a matter of time before land becomes scarcer and more valuable. With the growing world population increasing demanding more space, the chances of losing your money with your investment are slimmer than many other investments.

You Can Leverage Your Money With Land

One advantage with investing in land is that you get to negotiate its price. With the right negotiating skills, you can bargain and get a good buying price. This is especially true if you are dealing with a seller who is highly motivated in selling the piece of land, or who needs cash right away. If you are careful to buy your land at sale prices and not at the top of the market, you can really leverage your hard earned money.

Land Can Give You a High Return on Investment

If you know what you are doing and purchase land in the path of growth, you can buy parcels of land at a low price and sell them later for a much higher price. You may also develop the land and increase your asset's value as much as a hundredfold. You have heard about self-made billionaires who made it big because of real estate. This is one of the ways they made those billions.

You can Flip Land

Just like homes, you can flip land as well, without all the fix-up, open houses, and work. Plus, you can start "land flipping" for very little money. In our area the land prices are still historically low, and investors are now seeing the opportunity to buy land at rock bottom prices and flip it for a quick profit.

Land is an Easy-to-Understand Investment

I'm sure you have heard about accounting scandals involving the Stock Market and other such investments. You should not encounter this kind of complication with land investing. With a little bit of research, you can usually get a good picture of why property prices change, and at what rate.

With Land You Have Ownership

It goes without saying that there's an invaluable sense of pride that comes with the idea of 'ownership', and this is the peace of mind you get from investing in land. This also goes with the fact that land is tangible. You own something you can see, touch and use.

Land Has Practical Use

You can use your piece of land in a number of practical ways. You can develop the land, use it for recreation, subdivide it, or build a home on it. There are all kinds of possibilities. (Again, see Chapter 11 for some great ideas on how to use your land.)

With Land You Can Avoid Banks

With all the red tape and new banking laws, many people find it a lot simpler to avoid getting bank loans altogether. Often land is cheap enough that you can buy in cash. Even if you can't do that, owners will often carry the loan themselves with little down.

There is so much to gain and very little to lose when investing in land. Land is an extremely valuable resource with limited quantities available. If you purchase land in the path of growth, you can find yourself with a valuable asset that a lot of other people want to get their hands on. Investing in land, with the intent of holding on to the right property for the long-term, can make a lot more sense (and be a lot more profitable) than any other retirement vehicle out there. You can see why many rich real estate investors, who know what they are doing, use land investment as a secret strategy for building their wealth.

Chapter 2

The Second Secret of Wealthy Real Estate Investors: Know When to Buy and When to Sell

The most basic investing principal can be summed up with a quote by famous billionaire J. Paul Getty, "Buy when everyone else is selling and hold until everyone else is buying. That's not just a catchy slogan. It's the very essence of successful investing."

This sounds like simple advice, but it requires going against the direction the rest of the herd is moving. The goal is not to be one of the sheep. When the conventional wisdom of the times and everyone around you is telling you to do something exciting, you head the opposite direction.

Don't be a wolf either! Those are the people who take advantage of others and who break all the laws, if not legal, then moral. Wolves are the scammers and frauds— the Bernie Madhoff's— the ones who end up in jail, eventually. (I'll tell you more later about how to spot and avoid these guys in land sales.)

Instead of being a wolf or a sheep, you should try to be a sheep dog. Help others in the herd move up, while staying above the pack and not getting caught up in the herd mentality.

Another classic principal is "buy low and sell high" It is simple advice that works in most situations, but it is not always easy. Remember, you don't need to buy at the lowest price in the market and sell at the highest price— you just need to sell at a high enough price to make a profit. It's OK if someone else makes some profit on the purchase too, perhaps selling the land at a later date for even more money.

Don't beat yourself up if you didn't make as much money as you could have by perhaps selling at a different time. The goal is to sell with some profit, so you can find something else to invest in, continually moving up.

Look for land in areas where it is still a buyers' market, not a sellers' market. You may have to get outside of the area you live in to find this, but at any given time there is someplace where the prices of land are still low and people are still hesitant to buy. This is an area you should be looking into.

Land generally is not a liquid investment. You shouldn't purchase it with the idea that you can cash it in fast. (Although, I do need to mention that in the right markets and the right times, many land investors have used a buy and flip strategy.) But generally, land is usually more of a buy and hold investment. So this strategy of the wealthy is just as simple as buying when the prices are down and people want to sell, and selling when the prices go up and people want to buy.

Real estate runs in cycles. For more detailed information on how real estate cycles work I recommend reading Gary Keller's book, *Shift*. It was written for real estate agents, but contains valuable information about how real estate markets fluctuate on a regular basis.

Don't panic if you are not in the cycle you want. Just hang in there and wait. If it is not the time to sell your land, I have some ideas in chapter 9 on things to do with your land while you wait.

Chapter 3

The Third Secret of Wealthy Real Estate Investors: Have a Plan

So, now that you understand why buying land is a good investment, and how timing is so important, we need to talk about how to buy land that will bring you a profit.

The first thing you need to do is set your goals and have a plan of action. Approach land investment like a business, and any successful business needs a business plan. Know what you want to accomplish and have an end goal in mind before you buy. In the appendix of this book I have included a worksheet to help you build your investing plan. Take a look at it, but before you fill out the form, I want to go through the rest of the chapters in this book, so you will have a better idea of what you are doing when you build your plan. As you read through the book, begin to think about what you want to accomplish by investing in land.

Do you want to buy and hold for a long time? Do you want to wait until the prices go up and then sell for a profit? Do you want to quickly flip land? Do you want land to diversify your investments? Do you want to build a home on this land? Do you want the land for recreation purposes? Do you want to farm or ranch on your land? Do you want to develop it? Will you be building a retirement or an inheritance for your children?

Once you understand your "why" you can begin building a plan.

How do you pay for the land? Do you need to save money to buy in cash or for a down payment? Do you need to transfer money from another investment vehicle? Do you plan on buying with little or no money down?

What is your start date? Will you be searching on your own for FSBOs (For Sale By Owners) or using a real estate agent?

Where do you want to buy land? Do you know the location you are interested in? What criteria will you use to choose the land you will be buying? How will you determine what the best deal for you is?

It is important to have a goal and an action plan for your investment business. Don't worry if you don't know right now. I'll be discussing many of these issues and more in the chapters to come. By the end of this book you should be ready to start goal setting, planning and hopefully be ready to take action.

In this book I am going to go over some of the basics you need to purchase land and start your investment journey. If you want to do more than just buy a piece of land or two, and get into serious real estate investing, I highly recommend you read *The Millionaire Real Estate Investor* by Gary Keller. He explains how to become an expert in investing in real estate of all types.

Chapter 4

The Fourth Secret of Wealthy Real Estate Investors: Know Your Finances and Buying Options

It is time to consider how you plan on paying for your land investment. You should determine a budget for this. Consider whether you have cash available to pay for the land or at least for a down payment. There are several financing options for purchasing your land investment. If you will be financing the land, do you plan on doing that with a bank or with the owner, or perhaps a combination of cash, bank and owner financing?

Ways to Finance Your Land Purchase

Cash. Typically you will need cash for the earnest money with the offer and cash to pay for the property, or at least a down payment. There are ways that you can buy with little or no money down, but these kinds of deals take a lot more work and are harder to find. Most property purchases require at least some cash to start.

A few potential ways to get cash for a purchase or a down payment, if you don't have cash readily available, are:

- Take out a home equity loan on another property.
- Use the assets in your 401K to borrow money.
- Borrow the money from a friend or relative.
- Use inherited money.
- Sell non-real estate property, such as a car or RV.
- Exchange other real estate or use non-real estate property for a down payment. You will have more luck with this approach when talking to FSBO's.
- Do a 1031 Exchange and trade up on property you already own by taking advantage of this tax strategy. (It is important to

talk to your tax advisers and financial professionals to get information on how to property structure this so you can take advantage of the tax savings with this type of deal.)

Owner Carryback

The most common type of financing in land purchases is owner financing. When getting involved in this kind of contract, I highly recommend getting help from professionals such as real estate agents, attorneys, and escrow companies. Owner financing can be beneficial for all parties involved, if done properly and legally.

Some of the benefits of owner financing are that the terms can be negotiable and the credit requirements are usually less and often there may not even be a credit check.

There are two basic forms of owner financing:

Contract for Deed or Land Installment Contract

This type of contract allows the buyer to pay the land owner in installment payments over a predetermined period of time. There may be a balloon payment at the end of that period. The seller will retain the deed to the property until the debt for the property is paid in full.

This can be a good way for a buyer to purchase property, especially if the buyer doesn't have stellar credit or the cash to purchase the land upfront. The problem with this kind of contract comes if you have construction plans, which may be delayed until the rights to the land are fully transferred.

Mortgage/Trust Deed or Deed of Trust

With this type of contract, the seller will issue a deed to the buyer in return for a promissory note guaranteeing payment to the seller and a mortgage contract with a third party lender that acts as collateral for the promissory note. This makes things a little more complicated, but it works better if you are planning on an immediate building project.

Bank Loans

Another type of financing is bank loans. Land loans from banks are handled differently than home mortgage loans, and are usually more difficult to obtain. Raw land isn't typically something banks like to do, because the risk is higher for them that you will walk away from the loan. Banks usually charge a higher interest rate for land, want larger down payments, and offer more restrictive and shorter repayment terms. Banks also will usually want to see some kind of plan that shows that you will be improving the property. They are more likely to give a loan for a prime piece of real estate that can be used for commercial or residential development than for a piece of raw speculation land out in the middle of nowhere.

Down payments tend to be higher for raw land purchases because improvements such as houses that banks could use as collateral for the loan do not exist on raw land. Your down payment may range between 20-50% of the total price of the property.

You are more likely to get a bank loan if you are planning on building on the land soon, and you may qualify for a construction loan that will cover both the purchase of the land and the building project.

Improved property, zoned for your intended use, will be easier to get a loan for than unimproved property. Land purchased with immediate plans for construction is the easiest type of land loan to secure because the lender will be paid off when a mortgage is obtained on the structure.

The best banks to approach for lot or land financing would be local banks or credit unions. Local banks are part of the community and have a vested interest in seeing it grow, so they are more likely to give you a loan.

And, of course, the bank will want to review your personal credit history before giving you any loan.

If you are in a rural part of the country, and you are purchasing the land to develop a farm or ranch, you may be able to obtain specialized loans, such as those offered by the U.S. Department of Agriculture. They currently offer a program for low-income borrowers called Section 502 direct loans. These loans have relatively liberal lending terms and allow individuals to buy property with plans to make improvements needed to add a house to the lot.

Purchase Expenses

Remember to also plan in your budget for some of the common expenses that come with purchasing property. These include:

1. Due diligence. You will need to conduct research regarding the land you want to purchase. Some of this will be research you can do yourself. I will discuss this later in detail, but just know for now that this may also include expenses for perk tests, appraisals, well and water quality tests, land surveys, and other similar research.

2. Conversion costs. This includes the costs for anything you will need to do to convert the land for your intended use, such as constructing a home, running sewer lines, etc.

3. Carrying costs. This includes things such as loan repayment fees, the interest on your loan and any property taxes. (Unlike residences, raw land is not considered to depreciate for federal tax purposes, so you can't take a depreciation tax deduction for raw land.)

4. Deed preparation, affidavits, power of attorney and other documents. Depending on the deal and your state, you may have to hire an attorney to draft and execute documents.

5. Title conveyance, title search and title insurance.

6. Closing and escrow costs.

7. Recording and transfer fees. Besides recording the property sale with the county, this may include well transfer fees and septic transfer fees.

8. Financing costs. These are the fees associated with getting a bank loan, usually paid at closing. Sometimes these can sometimes be costly, so know what the fees are before you end up surprised at closing.

Final costs

Just how much money does this work out to in dollar terms?

As I mentioned earlier, if you are dealing with a property listed with a real estate broker, the seller will be paying a chunk of the down payment in brokerage commission, plus their closing costs, so they will want to get at least 20-25% down in cash.

Now add in closing costs, which often for a buyer can run from 3-5% of the purchase price, not including the due diligence costs.

You may actually need more on a small piece of property because some of the fees don't change with the price of the land and are close to the same, no matter what the land price is.

Some closing costs are fixed or very traditional in a certain area, but most everything in real estate is negotiable. The buyer can pay for all or some of the seller's costs if it helps get the deal done, or the same goes for the seller.

If you are not working with a real estate agent, talk to your escrow/title company and ask what they charge for closing costs to get a more exact idea of what you will need to pay.

Chapter 5

The Fifth Secret of Wealthy Real Estate Investors: Understand the Purchase Process

The Purchase Contract

An offer should be written as a purchase contract. If the seller does not want to accept the offer, they can sign the contract, explaining that a counter offer is now attached and then return it to the buyer with a counter offer addendum. The buyer signs the acceptance or signs that they are now sending a counter offer back to the seller. This goes on until everyone agrees and signs their agreement, or if no agreement is made the offer falls apart.

The contract for a land purchase should detail everything about the transaction, including listing the buyer, seller, agents, lender, and the title and/or escrow company.

The purchase contract also includes the address and legal description of the property, acceptance date, delivery date of proof of ownership, financing approval date and closing date, when the property will be recorded with the county and the buyer will take possession of the property. The purchase contract should also cover transaction terms, such as price, down payment, loan amount, financing terms and balance payable at closing. This can be in the original document or amended in counter offers and/or additional addendums.

Any addendums or counter offers will take precedence over what the original offer contract stated. For example, if just the purchase price of $25,000 was changed, the counter offer might state, "Purchase price to be $22,000. All other terms and conditions to be the same."

If the buyer is getting a loan, they generally need to show an approval letter from a bank or mortgage company. If the buyer is paying in cash, they usually will need to show a verification of funds before the seller approves the purchase contract.

If you are new to the real estate purchase process, I highly recommend you find a reliable attorney or real estate agent to help you navigate through this process, to be sure everything is legal and you are not being taken advantage of by someone who may know more about the process than you do.

Title Investigation

Title investigation begins once the contract is accepted and escrow is opened at a title company. During this period, a title company investigates public records to learn whether the owner owns the entire property or whether the owner has liens or judgments against the title. As long as a title search does not find any issues, the title company will produce title insurance, which guarantees the seller's right to sell the property.

If you are working with a lender, they will also order an appraisal to be sure the property is worth the value of the loan and will do a more thorough credit check of the buyer. It is possible that the bank or lending institution may decide at this point that the buyer doesn't qualify for the loan after all. If this is the case, it is usually written in the purchase contract that the deal falls apart (and is now over.)

Closing

In the past, the buyer, seller, applicable agents or attorneys and closing agents from the lender or title company, would all meet together at the scheduled closing. In today's new worldwide market, it isn't required for everyone to meet in person anymore. In a closing, the buyer and seller sign the applicable documents to agree to the terms of the financing and sale of the land. Although, this usually requires actual signatures (as opposed to e-signatures or faxed signatures), this can be done over long distances, with the help of mobile notaries.

Once the closing is done, the new ownership will be recorded in the applicable county records. This is usually taken care of by the title company. At this point the buyer can take possession of the property and is now the new owner.

Chapter 6

The Sixth Secret of Wealthy Real Estate Investors: Decide What Kind of Land is the Best for You to Buy

Types of Land

Land is usually considered to be vacant property with no permanent building, or with only a tear-down structure. There are many types of land available for you to consider for investment purposes. You should decide what kind of land you are looking for, and what your planned use will be, before you start your search. Below is a list of some of the major types of land you can purchase.

Residential Land and Homebuilding Lots

This is another popular investment strategy for both "buy & hold," as well as flipping investors. Again, the idea behind this is that we will always need shelter and good places to build more homes. These lots are usually found in the city or the suburbs. Investors should look for land that will likely be developed soon or in the near future, unless they are speculating for long term growth. In rapidly growing areas, specializing in buying and selling building lots can be lucrative.

This includes residential land for building your dream home, city lots in residential neighborhoods, land for small single-family starter homes, or even spacious lakefront and mountain estates.

In our area, because of the sporadic growth of the past, you can find lots right in the center of town, both single lots and multiple adjoining lots, with homes and apartments already developed around them.

Commercial and Industrial Land

This is land zoned to be developed for commercial, industrial and retail use. Commercial properties can range from small rural storefronts and restaurants to multimillion dollar retail centers. Industrial land is land to be developed into factories and for other industrial use, including alternative energy.

Commercial and industrial land is usually found in or just outside of cities and suburbs.

Some more ideas for commercial land include the hospitality industry and bed & breakfasts, golf courses, health care properties, and land for government buildings.

Working with commercial property is a more complex investment technique that may not be best suited for the beginner in real estate, unless you are willing to put in some time to learn more about commercial property and its valuation. You will need to take into account the income potential of the property, historical revenue, cash flow with owner perks removed, and much more. It's better to enter this specialization carefully after spending some time in the real estate business in land or residential property markets.

Farms and Agricultural Land

This includes many types of land, ranging from small, organic farms in the Pacific Northwest to large farms in the nation's breadbasket. This also includes dairy farms, horse farms, aquaculture, poultry farms, orchards and vineyards. This is a popular investment in today's market. The idea is that if the economy falls apart, we will always need food and farmland. Usually this land is found in the country or just outside of cities. With farmland, you can hold it by farming it yourself or renting it out, or you can buy it on a discount and flip it (depending on the situation). Or you can convert it to something else, like a housing development.

Ranches

Land for sale used by farmers and ranchers for their livestock, ranging from small pastures used for smaller livestock production, to large multipurpose ranches with many acres of owned or leased land.

Recreational Land and Vacation Property

This may be land utilized for various purposes, including camping, fishing, hiking, vacation and other recreational uses. This can include mountain property, high desert recreation land, desert property, river front, beach front and lake front properties.

Recreation property is very popular in our area of the high desert of Northern Arizona, partly because of the cooler climate, and partly because of the available unlived-in open space and beautiful country. Seligman, Kingman, Peach Springs and Ash Fork are only a few hours away from some of the hottest cities in the US, Las Vegas, Phoenix and LA, and make a great escape from the heat.

Hunting Land

This is a specific type of recreational land that can be leased or otherwise used to hunt game and fish. Depending on the local laws, this can be game found naturally on the property, or it can be privately stocked.

Waterfront properties

In our area, we have the Colorado River, with all its playground fun, easily in reach from large cities. Lake Havasu City, Parker, Bullhead City have some wonderful waterfront and water view lots available. Although these properties can be recreational, many people live in these properties and lake front communities year round.

Speculation Land

Raw, vacant and undeveloped land an investor will buy and hold, with the idea that hopefully the price will increase later. Some people buy this kind of land to build a retirement portfolio or to pass on to their heirs as an inheritance.

Mineral Rights

Some people want land so they can search for gold, silver and other precious gems and minerals. Buying and selling mines and mineral rights can also be a lucrative business, if you know what you are doing. This is another popular investment technique in our area, where minerals are plentiful. Check into your state's laws on this. It can vary greatly.

Water rights

Some states sell water rights separately from the land. In these states there are investors who specialize in buying and selling water rights. Again, check into your state's laws on this.

Other Land Types

This includes properties which do not fit into any of the above categories, such as foresting properties, conservation land, timeshares, and parking.

Another way that you may hear land categorized is brownfield land, greenfield land, and greyfield land.

Brownfield Land

This is land that was used for industrial purposes sometime in the past and is now not being used or has been abandoned. It is possible this land has been contaminated with chemicals or dangerous waste, so make sure you know this before you proceed to buy it. It is possible to clean it up, but check into how much that will cost and what regulations you need to follow before you purchase this kind of land.

Greenfield Land

This is what it sounds like, land that growing plants are on. There might be woods or trees on it. It can be wild growth or a planned greenbelt area that keeps urban sprawl at bay.

Greyfield Land

Land that was developed in a non-industrial way at some time in the past, perhaps with homes, and now it is partially used, abandoned or underused.

Chapter 7

The Seventh Secret of Wealthy Real Estate Investors: Finding Good Land Deals

So, by now you should have a good of how you are going to purchase your land. The next step is to start looking for good land and good deals.

When purchasing land as an investment one of the main things you should keep in mind is to look for land that is in the path of growth. If you are looking for land to increase in value, find an area that is beginning to expand. Are there any homes or developments nearby? Are there builders and developers working around you? Does the land have any utilities or improvements? How is the access to the property? Most of these issues will be discussed in the Due Diligence chapter, but start watching for it as you search for your land to buy.

There are many ways of searching for good property. I have found that some of the best places to begin your search are:

People You Know

Ask around and let people in your circle know that you are interested in buying land. This is the first way you should start you search. Someone you know might know someone else. Some of the best land deals come from acquaintances or friends of acquaintances and/or family. These people often just want to get rid of a property quickly, and don't really care if they get full market value for it. Or they may be more generous with terms and down payment because they know and trust you more.

Online Searches

More than 90% of real estate buyers today search for property online before buying. With all the consumer real estate websites out there, real estate buyers now are more educated and have more information at their fingertips than buyers have ever had before. On the other hand, there is a confusing inundation of information that makes it hard to find exactly what you want and need. Not to mention that not all the information online is correct, and scams abound.

Buyers searching online without any professional help need to be savvy and know what they are doing. For first time buyers, or buyers who have little experience, it is important to be sure you have the professional help you need to buy without getting into trouble.

To be honest, I don't recommend any one online source for information. All of them have their strengths and their problems. I use at least a couple of sources when I look for property or comps (comparisons of similar properties and prices) online for myself or my clients.

Online Real Estate Sites

Let's talk a little about using Zillow.com, Trulia.com, Homes.com, Realtor.com and other online real estate websites. They have their negatives and their positives, but it's important to understand how they can be used and when you should not rely on them.

First of all, let's look at Realtor.com. This is a site I use frequently, but it also has limitations. This website comes from the Realtor® organization. In it is a collection of every listing from every MLS and Realtor® in the United States.

A Multiple Listing Service or MLS, according to Wikipedia.org, "is a suite of services that enables real estate brokers to establish contractual offers of compensation (among brokers), facilitates cooperation with other broker participants, accumulates and disseminates information to enable appraisals, and is a facility for the orderly correlation and dissemination of listing information to better serve broker's clients, customers and the public. A multiple listing service's database and software is used by real estate brokers in real estate... representing sellers under a listing contract to widely share information about properties with other brokers who may represent potential buyers or wish to cooperate with a seller's broker in finding a buyer for the property or asset."   In other words, to put it simply, it's a place where agents and brokers share their listings with each other.

Realtor.com does not include any FSBO (for sale by owner) sales or foreclosures unless they have found a way to get into their local MLS. Some discount real estate companies will list homes for sale by owner for a discount fee, which basically just puts them in the MLS. The owners still have to do most of the work themselves, as far as promotions.

Realtor.com is a search site that is a compilation of local MLS listings from agents and brokers who belong to the Realtor® organization. Not all real estate agents are Realtors®, but more than half are. Realtor.com is a good resource for searching for homes and land that are listed by agents, especially when you need to access more than one MLS area. It also has fairly accurate data, since the agents entered the info themselves. It is not the best, in my opinion, for specific area searches and map searches. Also it is not the place to go if you are looking for properties listed with non-Realtor® brokers, FSBOs or foreclosures that are not listed on the local MLS.

Every local area has its own multiple listing service, usually called MLS for short. (And no, with this MLS we are not talking about soccer). There is no one major public MLS list, except for Realtor.com. Most local MLS organizations do have public searches, which don't give as much information as the real estate agent section, but can still be useful. Do a web search for your city or county and see if the local multiple listing service has a public search you can use.

Zillow and Trulia are actually now owned by the same organization, but they are independently operated and still seem to compete against each other for adverting. They both use "public information" to fill their databases, including tax records and MLS information. This public information has been disputed, especially by Realtors® and MLS companies, since part of the information comes from propriety information that the Realtors® have paid for. At this point in time, courts have upheld that the listing data stored in a MLS's database is the proprietary information of the broker who has obtained the listing agreement with the seller of the property.

Pros: Zillow and Trulia include information that may not be in Realtor.com, such as FSBOs and Foreclosures. You can also find out more about properties, such as when it was sold last and for how much. Also both give an estimate on the price of the property. They also have great map and area searches

Cons: Be very careful about taking the information you find on these sites as facts. I find errors all the time on these sites, and even if they are my listings, I have a hard time getting them corrected. Agents have little or no control over what these sites put up as "facts." Also the estimate (or Zestimate) is really rough. They don't really take into account all the factors that a good estimate or appraisal will, especially if the home is custom or outside of a tract home area. I find that typically the price estimate on Zillow or Trulia can be from 25% to 50% off of what a good estimate will be on custom homes and country properties.

Also they are not always up to date. I find that especially true with foreclosures, which may be years behind in their data. So these tools may be good for starting and even refining your search, but verify all information before you take it literally.

Classified Ads and FSBOs

When searching for property there is always the "old fashioned" way —using the newspaper, local ad papers, and other printed sources. This is being used less and less, but still is something to consider. Often FSBOs (For Sale By Owners) and real estate agents who are less computer savvy, or more used to doing things the old way, will use these methods, so it may be worth you time to check out.

Online classified advertisement sites, the biggest being Craigslist, are also worth checking out. Certainly, there are many good properties listed on Craigslist, although the ads are not organized much and can be cluttered. I've found that a large portion of them in our area are offered by FSBOs, and this may be a great way to find FSBO properties.

As a real estate agent, I can tell you that Craigslist can be a pain for someone in a commercial business. Craigslist doesn't like businesses and seem to do their best to discourage business owners. They don't like multiple ads, they insist the advertiser stay only in their small area, and they don't allow links and other useful marketing tools. Also, if the market in a certain area is very competitive, I've found that other competing agents will mark my legal ads as spam, and then Craigslist put my ads into no-man's-land where they can't be found, and eventually may get me banned from Craigslist all-together. There are ways to deal with all these things, but as a successful real estate agent, often it is not worth the time and effort, when other methods of marketing may work just as well or better. If you want to see what property is for sale in an area, you may not see a large representation of real estate brokers' listings on Craigslist. One of the other real estate sites would be better for this.

There are also some things you should be very careful about when using Craigslist and other online classified ad sites. Craigslist and online classified ad sites have become well known for real estate scams. One of the most popular is the rental scam, where a scammer finds a home that is for sale and puts up an ad on Craigslist for renting out the property at an amazing deal. They take the down payment from the renter in advance to "save the property for them," and when the would-be renter tries to move into the property, they find the scammer has run off with their money and the property was never a rental to begin with.

Land scams include advertising worthless property with false pictures and information. If you follow my advice for doing your "due diligence" it will be much harder for you to fall prey to these scammers who take advantage of ignorant buyers.

Using a Real Estate Agent

What I see is that much in the real estate market has changed in the last 20-30 years. In the past Realtors® held all the information for searches and about properties. You needed them to help you find what you wanted. Now there is so much information for real estate buyers to find online and buyers have become very savvy researchers using online methods, some wonder what is the point of using a real estate agent for purchasing property, or even for selling property?

Maybe not much as far as finding a property. You can certainly find real estate for sale without a real estate agent, and you can put your property up for sale easily online by owner. And land is easy to find and visit with gps and online mapping programs. With land you don't need a Realtor® to have a key for the door.

But the majorities of listings are still in the MLS, and as such usually have contracts with real estate brokers. This means that most of the time you can't deal directly with the owner. You will still need to go through the real estate broker who is acting as the seller's agent. For most listed properties, even if you somehow made a deal directly with the owner, the owner will still need to pay the real estate agent their commission, as per the contract.

So what do real estate agents do to earn their commission now, if most buyers find their property online?

To start, real estate agents have access to the MLS and can often give you information that you can't find online.

Also, the role of the real estate agent has changed since the 80's and 90's. There are so many new rules and regulations in real estate purchase and financing now, that it's a maze for the average person who just wants to buy a property. A real estate agent should be able to help you navigate through all this red tape— city and county ordinances, rules and regulations, as well as state and federal government requirements. The Dodd Frank laws, which are continually adding new regulations, have changed much of the landscape in real estate and financing, and will continue to do so.

Real estate agents should also be good negotiators, who will be a less emotional and more experienced party to deal with the other side of the deal. They know the now much more complicated process of making offers, dealing with lenders, dealing with title and escrow companies, and dealing with local governments. A good real estate agent can help you get through this complicated process with much more ease.

Ask your agent to help you verify the information on land you are interested in. As a buyer, using a real estate agent doesn't cost you a thing, so why not use this resource.

If you are still totally against using an agent or broker, be sure you run your deal through a lawyer and/or escrow company. They are well worth the fees you pay to make sure you are doing everything correctly and not violating any laws.

Real estate agents are a particularly good option when your search is somewhere out-of-state or far away from your current residence. Also, real estate agents are required to mention things like easements and highway improvements. An easement grants someone other than the property owner the right to use a tract of land, such as giving neighbors road access or the ability to ride a horse through the land. This limits how the land can be developed, so it's important you are aware of this before buying the property. A real estate agent may also be able to tell you whether there may be any future zoning plans that could affect your own plans.

Tax Lien Sales

There are some people out there who make a lot more money selling books and programs on tax lien sales than they do on the real estate. It is not as easy as some of these guru's make it sound. Although you can make money at this, depending on where you are located, and maybe get title to some land, you really need to know what you are doing. Know the land's worth and understand the state and local area's laws and customs before you bid. Visit the property and check it out in person. If you get to know the owners and their situation, that is even better.

When you purchase a tax lien at an auction, you pay off the lien for the delinquent taxes (usually several years' worth) from the county or other government entity. There are two main ways you can get property, depending on your state— with a Tax Lien Certificates and with the Collector's Deeds.

In states where you get a Tax Lien Certificate, you have just purchased the lien not the property, paying off the past due taxes. Sometimes with a Tax Certificate the owners are given a time period where they can pay off the lien to you and recover their property. Some people just make money on the interest charged on these tax liens when they get paid for them, not on getting the property. They may or may not end up owning the property.

In states where the buyer receives a Collector's Deed, it is easier and quicker to end up getting the property, but even if you receive a Collector's Deed for the property, instead of a Tax Certificate, you still don't have clear title to the land and you will need to start the process of clearing the title. If there are other lien holders, they may be offered the chance to pay off the tax lien and take title to the property instead of you. Often this process takes several years before you can get the title.

It is possible that the owner of a parcel could fight someone in court to get the land back. This is why most title companies won't insure property that comes by a Collector's Deed. There are legal steps you can go through to get a Quiet-title, but you will need an attorney and to spend some more money to do this.

All in all, I suggest caution if you want to acquire property at tax lien auctions, and again, become an expert in the process before you start. It is not an area to get into if you don't know what you are doing.

Auctions

Auctions can be another easy way to find land to buy. There are live auctions and now there are many online auctions, including eBay, which are becoming increasingly popular.

As with all real estate purchases, you need to do your homework before you buy. With auctions this is even more important. I've often seen property listed at online auctions that are much higher than property I have listed in the same area. I've also seen property that was misleading. The pictures were from the "area" not the property itself. In our area, they talk a lot about how close the land is to gambling in Las Vegas or Laughlin, or near the Grand Canyon, but don't say much about the piece of worthless dirt in the middle of nowhere (hours away from Vegas or Grand Canyon) that you are buying.

You can still find some good deals at auctions. Again, the key is education and knowing what you are doing. Thoroughly research the area where the land is located. Find out why that particular piece of land is up for auction.

Often cash is needed for auctions, although some auctions are just for the down payment. The rest of the purchase price is the same. Some auction sites also will also allow owner carry loans. Be sure you read the entire auction listing. There are many scams out there and auctions are one way they try to snag you.

Land Development Websites

There are also many land development websites online that are put together by the owners and developers to sell their property. Be careful. Scams are often sold this way. On the other hand, many of these websites are legitimate, and lots of decent land has been purchased this way. Many of these websites offer owner financing as well, so this may be a good way for a buyer to purchase land who has only a little cash to put down.

Since these sites are put together to sell, even though they may be licensed agents or brokers, I suggest you find a real estate agent to represent you in a purchase, so your interests and needs are taken care of. It doesn't cost you anything so take advantage of this resource. And, of course, go see the land you are about to buy, to be sure that what they say and what you are buying is the same thing.

Talk to Local Owners

Another way to find good land for sale is to pick the area you really want to buy land in, whether it is an area you want to live or an area you think is not selling right now and will have good inflation value in the future. Once you have your area, visit and talk to current residents. Contact the local HOA leadership and talk to them as well. Ask questions about the area. Ask if they know anyone who wants to sell and see if they would give those people your number as a potential buyer.

Letter Writing

Also, you can write letters to everyone in the development, asking them if they are interested in selling their land, or if they know someone who is. Be ready to answer with an offer that you have in mind, because they are sure to ask, if they reply. In our state, you can find get the land owners mailing information online. Some states have stronger privacy rules, so that may be harder to reach owners this way. You can see if a local title company can help you out with a mailing list. It helps if you have a good relationship with one of the agents at the company, and use them for your escrows.

Research Evictions, Bank Foreclosures, and Tax Sales

Another way to find land seller leads is to research evictions, bank foreclosures and tax sales. If the property has a tax lien or they are behind payments on it, the owner might be willing to sell it to you and have you pay off the debt instead, if they can make a little money on it, instead of just letting it go for nothing, because of the money owed that they can't pay. Watch for ads in newspapers that announce foreclosure sales.

There are websites that just deal in real estate foreclosures. Some auction sites sell foreclosures as well, so there is a large resource online if you have the cash to pick up some of these deals. Some real estate agents compile lists of foreclosures as well.

Part 2: Doing Your "Due Diligence"

Chapter 8

The Eighth Secret of Wealthy Real Estate Investors: Avoid Poor Choices

People often just make poor choices in buying land. The land may not be what they thought it was, because they didn't do enough research. I find that people are trying to sell land they bought because it turns out it that the CC&R's (Covenants, Conditions & Restrictions set by the developer or home owners association) won't allow them to build what they wanted to build. Or perhaps their land doesn't have very good road access, or it has a huge wash across it. Doing your due diligence will go a long way towards helping you avoid costly mistakes. (See Chapter 9 for more information on this.)

Avoiding Land Scams

There are many land scams going on in the United States and all across the world. You don't want to lose your hard earned money by getting caught up in them.

I've heard many stories about how people lost money on land, especially in the areas of Nevada and Arizona, where I have worked in real estate and where many land scams have historically abounded. I met one man whose grandfather bought land in Arizona back during World War II and when the heirs wanted to sell it recently, research showed that all roads to the property have long disappeared and there has been no development what-so-ever in the area. The land now is worth about the same amount that the grandfather paid almost 80 years ago.

One of the scams going on is the classic telemarketer "land investment" scam. Often these scammers will send unsuspecting buyers a card asking them to call in and claim their prize because they have won land or something related. Of course, they always want money up front, and usually try to get the buyer's credit card information.

With the rise of the internet, many land scams have gone "high-tech" and are sold on the web and auction websites like eBay to unsuspecting buyers, especially those who are out of the area and unable to visit the property. Often these lots being sold are advertised with photos showing running water, green trees and green grass — things that simply don't exist in that particular isolated desert location. The ones in our area also show pictures of "near-by" Las Vegas or the Grand Canyon, which could be hundreds of miles away.

There are also common online scams where the "seller" copies and advertises a legitimate listing of land for sale, and when contacted, sends the buyer to a bogus escrow website to deposit their money, and then once the money has been handed over, neither the fake seller nor the escrow company is ever heard from again.

Online sites say they just provide the place to advertise properties. They don't monitor what properties are being sold. Sites like eBay, the world's largest auction marketplace, which lists and auctions properties in its real estate section, really just facilitates connections between people. Legally eBay can't sell real estate, and the actual transaction happens directly between the buyer and seller. This is why it is important for land buyers and potential land investors to be careful and educate themselves.

The Right Land but the Wrong Time

Timing is everything in real estate speculation. I recently spoke to a woman who bought parcels of land near a huge up-and-coming development about 10 years ago. This development was highly marketed, and was supposed to be huge, with plans for thousands of homes and large golf courses. But then the real estate collapse of 2008-9 hit, and everything fell apart. The developer filed bankruptcy and nothing came of the development. So, 10 years later, when this land owner called me to sell her land, she was surprised to find out it was worth about 10% of what she had originally paid for it.

It is important to buy land at the right time and in the right place. And you can't always control what will happen with real estate speculation, but there are a few secrets the rich use to make more informed decisions on when, where and how to buy real estate and land.

For instance, now might be a better time to buy the land in that development that fell apart. Perhaps someone will come along and resurrect the project. Now would be the time to pay one tenth the price and get a good return if and when the development is brought back to life. Remember, the rich buy when everyone is selling and sell when everyone is buying.

Chapter 9

The Ninth Secret of Wealthy Real Estate Investors: Research is Everything!

About Due Diligence

"Due Diligence" is the legal term for what a buyer needs to check out before buying something, especially something expensive like real estate.

According to Investopedia, "Due diligence (DD) is an investigation or audit of a potential investment. Due diligence serves to confirm all material facts in regards to a sale. Generally, due diligence refers to the care a reasonable person should take before entering into an agreement or a transaction with another party."

Doing your research and due diligence is the biggest way to avoid getting caught in a land scam. The maxim *caveat emptor* or "buyer beware" is never more important than when buying land and real estate of any kind.

It is, of course, of utmost importance that you find out if you can do what you want to do with the land you are planning to buy. As an example, if you want to put a manufactured home on the land, you will want to be sure the zoning and development rules allow this.

It is the buyer's responsibility to thoroughly check out and inspect real estate property before committing to buy it. This is the "Buyer Beware" caution for real estate.

Buying land or any real estate for that matter is an investment risk. There are no guarantees that the price will increase. There may also be hidden problems of which buyer is unaware. This is why this period of "due diligence" is so important (and legally required.) Do not ignore this or wave your right for inspections.

It is not the seller's responsibility to supply this information to the buyer. The seller is required (at least in our state - or depending on the state?) to disclose what they know about the property. Perhaps it is in a flood zone or a neighbor has an easement through the property to reach their property. But if the seller doesn't know about it, they are usually not liable for something they don't know. I find sellers every week who inherit a piece of land from a relative and have never seen the land and have no idea about anything to do with it. And, let's be realistic, there are sellers out there who will claim they didn't know about an issue, even if they did.

It is also not your real estate agent or the listing agent's responsibility to do your due diligence and research for you. It is nice if they supply some of the information for you, but please double check the information they do supply. I have often seen errors in listing information as well.

Because of this very issue, and the fact that America is so "sue happy," it is not in the real estate agent's best interest to supply research and do the due diligence for you. Realtors® are specialists in sales, not in any other areas. Talk to or hire a professional who is a specialist in their field to get the correct information you need to make informed decisions.

In the end, it is up to you as a buyer to check out all the pertinent information on the piece of property you want to buy, and double check any information you receive from other non-professionals or sellers.

Your Realtor® should give you a list of professional providers who can assist you with finding the information you need. If you are buying on your own, or your real estate agent is new to dealing with land (or just doesn't want to work) you may have to find these professionals on your own.

Where Should You Start With Due Diligence?

In the appendix of this book is a basic (although not exhaustive) "Due Diligence List" of things you may want to research before you buy your land. I've actually seen lists with over 100 items on it, and each purchase and development area/county/municipality is different, so this is just some of the basic information most buyers look at. Before you begin to panic or hyperventilate, I will explain more in this chapter about how to do some of the research yourself online. And in the next chapter, Chapter 10, I explain how to find good professionals you can hire to help you with your due diligence.

1. Find price comparisons of similar properties

Make sure that what you are paying for the property is a fair price. If you are using a real estate broker, ask him or her to give you comps for similar properties in the area. If you are not using a broker, then you will need to do this research on your own. Do online searches on Zillow.com, Trulia.com, LandandFarm.com, Landwatch.com and Realtor.com. Try to find properties that are the most similar. Be careful of trusting the "Zestimate" or other website quick real estate price estimate. (See my information on using Zillow and Truila in Chapter 7 for more on this subject.)

2. Physical Land Use Due Diligence

Boundaries and surveys. I always suggest getting a survey done to find out what the exact boundaries of the land are. I have seen "errors" in fencing and even buildings that encroached into their neighbor's lot. If left long enough, these encroachments could eventually end up becoming part of their property. Don't let someone take away what is rightfully your land just because you didn't know.

Aerial maps and topographical maps. You can learn a lot from maps and aerial satellite images.

Online at USGS Explorer (http://earthexplorer.usgs.gov/) you can find historic aerial photos that may show past land use patterns, farming practices, land management and natural areas.

For USGS Topographical Maps that you can search for by address and download, go to http://nationalmap.gov/ustopo/index.html

Most local counties have a version of a GIS mapping system online, where you can find your property by the address, parcel number or possibly even the owner's name. According to Wikipedia, GIS or a geographic information system is "a system designed to capture, store, manipulate, analyze, manage, and present all types of spatial or geographical data." In other words, you can find all kinds of good information put together on a GIS site. To find your area, try a Google search with your county's name and GIS, for instance, "Yavapai County AZ GIS".

And then there is always Google Satellite Maps at www.maps.google.com.

Slope and elevation. A photo or a satellite map gives you a place to start, but it doesn't really show the slope and elevation of the land very well. You really need to see the land in person to get a good idea of what it really looks like. Look for low spots and areas where there is standing water or evidence of past standing water. Is there any evidence of erosion, gullies or washes?

I almost bought a piece of land in the mountains of Utah many years ago. Even though it had an amazing view, I changed my mind when I visited the land saw that it was almost all a crumbling slope that looked like a very dangerous place to build a cabin. I suspected it needed a lot of modifications to build on it, so I backed out of buying the place. Looking back, I should have had an engineer or geologist check it out to see if it could have been a buildable, and if so, how much work would it be, and I would have known for sure. Anyway, I did discover the problem by visiting the land in person, which made all the difference.

Vegetation. Know what is growing on your land. Is there anything that could be considered protected? Are there any invasive species of weeds? If you have timber, do you have the rights to cut it down if you wish? Do you need a permit?

Water flow, flood areas and washes. You might be able to see this from a satellite map, but again, it's easier to understand when you visit the land in person. Consider consulting with a geologist or engineer if there are potential issues. Also check to see if the general area is in a flood plain. (I'll tell you how you can do this yourself in the next chapter.)

If there is a creek or a pond on the property, take note of the water content and quality. Is it a seasonal flow or does it run all year? Is there any upstream pollution? Do cattle or livestock have access to the water?

Mineral and Water Rights. In some areas the water rights and mineral rights are sold separately from the land, and in some areas they go with the land. Know how it works with the property you are buying.

Environmental reports and issues. Is the property located in, or does it have a protected area, such as a wetland delineation? Are there any protected and /or endangered animal species studies going on in that area that you need to be aware of? This can stop building and development if there are, so you need to know for sure.

Geotechnical and soils report, perc tests. When you visit the land, take note of the soil condition and texture. Consider taking a shovel and checking how hardpan the ground is. Is there any organic matter that can be used for growing plants or crops?

If you want to build or put in a septic system you may need to get soil reports and perc tests, as well as permits from your local authorities. In Arizona, developers who sell more than 6 lots need to make a Public Development Report (a state law that has been enacted to protect consumers from land development scams.) If you are a part of a development that has a public report already, you can find much of the information on soil and perc tests as well as other information you need in the report. Sometimes these reports are old and out of date, but they may still give you some good information. You can find public report information for Arizona on the Arizona Department of Real Estate website at:
http://services.azre.gov/publicdatabase/Default.aspx

3. Legal, Development and Regulatory Issues

Talk to your city and/or county's Planning and Development Department about these issues:

Zoning Verification. You will want to confirm that a property's zoning is compatible with how you would like to use the land.

Find out how the properties around your land are zoned. Ask if there are any future changes, building projects or developments planned for the area. Is there anything that can affect the view from your property?

City and County Ordinances and Building Regulations.

These are particularly important to know if you plan on building or improving your lot, but they may also affect the price and ability to sell your lot later.

What is the Approval and Permitting Process? What are the permitted and conditional uses of the land? Are there any Restrictions in land use or in the location of home? Is manufactured housing allowed? Is RV parking allowed?

Find the Tax Information.

What will you have to pay the local authorities for taxes on your land? Some counties and states publish this information online at the County Assessor's website. Some states have privacy laws that make this research harder to find, and you will need to talk to your County Assessor Office.

4. Improvements

Access to utilities and utility verification. Are there any water, septic or sewer maps for the area? Find out who the local utility companies are and contact them.

Fences. If the property is fenced, be sure the fences are actually on the property and not encroaching on a neighbor's lot.

Sheds and outbuildings. Do any outbuildings have the proper permits? It is common in our area to find that sheds and other buildings were erected without any permits. Is there any water or wind damage to the outbuildings? What outbuildings will stay with the land purchase and what do the sellers or you want removed. Always get that in writing in your purchase contract.

Wells and water storage tanks. Does the property have a well or a water storage tank? How deep is the well? How safe is the water? Does the pump system work? If its farmland, does the land have an irrigation infrastructure, such as a well, pump, mainline, etc.

Septic systems. Does the property have a septic system? Does it work properly? Does it need to be pumped? What are the laws in the area about property transfer? In our area it is a state law that the septic system must be pumped when a property is sold. Will the property need a septic system in the future to build? Will the municipality require the property to be hooked up to the city sewer system in the future?

Other improvements. Are there any other improvements you should know about and check into? One example would be an RV hookup.

Equipment. Is there any other equipment or machinery on the property that needs to be removed, or that you can possibly include in the sale?

Land management. Has the land been actively managed or has it been neglected?

Environmental concerns. Is there trash, old fuel tanks or chemical dumping areas on the property that will need to be cleaned up?

5. Access and Roads

Road access, offsite road improvements & onsite road circulation. Know what kind of access there is to your land. Is it close to a main road? How much traffic does the road get and will there be any road noise? How accessible is the land? Do you need a four wheel drive vehicle to get to it?

Future road information. Will there be any road development any time soon? Is a highway planned in the area? It can make a big difference, either positive or negative, to your land use.

Road maintenance. Find out whom, if anyone, is maintaining the roads. It might be the county, the developer, or a homeowners association.

6. Property Owners Associations

Land Development Information and Regulations. Your land may be included in a homeowner's association (HOA) or property owners association (POA). A HOA is defined by Wikipedia as "a homeowner association (HOA) is a corporation formed by a real estate developer for the purpose of marketing, managing, and selling of homes and lots in a residential subdivision." Investopedia defines it as "A homeowner's association (HOA) is an organization in a subdivision, planned community or condominium that makes and enforces rules for the properties in its jurisdiction."

Property owners associations (POAs) and homeowners associations (HOAs) are similar to each other, but there are a few things that set them apart. One main difference is that with HOAs there needs to be some kind of home on the property. POAs on the other hand are more about the land itself and can be in a development with only vacant lots. Sometimes POAs are started around a physical feature such as a golf course or lake.

Homeowners associations usually have membership rules with the goal of maintaining standards within a residential community, such as requiring lawn upkeep, or not allowing manufactured homes in the community. Members are typically charged a membership fee which is used to maintain community property such as parking areas, common lawn areas, playgrounds and pools.

Property owners associations are similar, but are looking at a bigger picture than just the neighborhood. For instance, many POAs offer education and networking opportunities. Some allow members to join who are business owners and/or connected to the real estate industry and not just the property owners in the development. POAs often have less rules and regulations, and some have none at all. Often POAs have much smaller fees as well.

Land in a development can have homeowners associations, property owners associations, or neither. Some people love HOAs and POAs and some people hate them. It all depends on personalities, past experience and what the particular HOA is like. When I mention to some buyers that a piece of land in a development has an HOA or a POA I often get a negative response. But in land, especially here in Arizona, a POA is often a very good thing. Because of the abundance of land scams here in the past, POAs and HOAs were often formed by the homeowners themselves to protect their rights as property owners and to be sure they get the amenities they were promised.

Often these land POAs have much fewer rules and regulations, and are nowhere near the cost, compared to HOAs or PUDs for home and condo developments in the city. (According to Wikipedia.org, "a planned unit development (PUD), is a type of building development... it is a designed grouping of both varied and compatible land uses, such as housing, recreation, commercial centers, and industrial parks, all within one contained development or subdivision.") Many of the land POAs in our area have a once-a-year fee that is much less than a condo owner in the city pays per month. I've seen fees as low as $75 a year. Most often this fee goes towards road maintenance, and sometimes a community well and/or trash pickup. This could very well be something that will add value to your land.

Usually there are few rules, although some communities have more rules than others. You need to find the community HOA or POA that is the best fit for you. I have also found that in our area POAs are often a social club as well. When owners live far apart out in an area that is 30 miles or more from the nearest city, they tend to form close bonds and help take care of each other.

Find out if your land has an HOA or a POA. It is very important for buyers to find out what the HOA or POA is like in the area in which they are interested in purchasing property. Be sure you get a copy of any covenants and restrictions that may limit the use of your property. Read them carefully to be sure they are something you can live with before you buy your land.

What are the community amenities? What are the costs and fees? Is the HOA mandatory or is it voluntary? What kind of maintenance and appearance rules do they have?

Finding the HOA rules and bylaws is not always easy. First ask the seller or the seller's agent. If they don't have a copy, often you can get a copy of the HOA rules and regulations by giving the association board a call. Sometimes you can find this information online if you search for the development or the association's name and website. Also a local title company may be able to help find this information. Some states have copies on their Department of Real Estate website. If you can't find them anywhere, ask your local title company. They may have a copy or be able to find you a copy.

7. Title Issues

I think it is important to go through a title company when buying real estate and get title insurance. This way you can be sure about the correct ownership of the property. You can find out if there are any liens and financial issues. You will learn about any official easements, dedications and encroachments on the property. And you will get a title insurance policy with copies of all exceptions.

Chapter 10

The Tenth Secret of Wealthy Real Estate Investors: Utilize the Experts

Getting Help and Advice from Experts and Professionals

When working on your due diligence, it is always a good idea to call in experts who can help you evaluate your purchase and answer important questions for you. Here is a list of the major professionals you may want to consider consulting with:

Lawyers

Depending on the state or country you are in, real estate lawyers may be a necessity, or at the least, very valuable for your land purchase. They can help assist you with the buying process and contracts, as well as the planning permission process.

In most cases, though, lawyers are not needed for most real estate transactions. Typically, real estate agents who are used to dealing in land can help you purchase property. They use standard contract forms and are familiar with the process. The escrow/title company should be able to help you as well.

There are a few states, however, that require a lawyer to prepare the purchase documents, do title searches and close the deal. A few other states require an attorney to be involved in some aspect of the sale. Check with your state real estate commission to find out if your state is one of these.

You should consider getting a lawyer if your situation is complicated, such as with a probate or foreclosure, you are buying or selling property with a non-family member, or you are doing something unusual (such as a seller helping a buyer get a loan) and need special language for the purchase contract. Also, if you are concerned about some of the language in your contracts, you may want to have an attorney look the documents over.

And whether a lawyer, a real estate agent, or someone else is helping you out, make sure that you actually read everything you sign. Be sure to ask questions if there's something you don't understand.

Real Estate Agents and Brokers

In my state, Arizona, we use real estate agents and not lawyers to help with the real estate buying process. But even if your state uses lawyers, real estate agents can be a valuable asset to help you find and buy your land. Realtors® have access to databases and information searches that you may not have. They know the area and should know, or be able to find out about, the regulations and zoning rules. They have standardized contracts drawn up by teams of lawyers in that state that you can use. Real estate agents are familiar with the buying and contracting process in the area where you want to buy your land.

A good real estate agent will be an expert at negotiating deals, so you don't need to get personally involved in dealing with a cranky seller. An agent should also have contacts with professionals, such as inspectors, mortgage loan officers, engineers, title companies, and maybe even local government officials who can help you with permits and planning.

Remember, you don't need to use the seller's agent for your purchase, and it's really not recommended. A real estate agent is a legal "agent," which means that that they are required to be loyal to the client they are representing. That means that a seller's agent's loyalty is first and foremost to their listing client, and not with the buyer who contacts them about the property. That agent may be happy to facilitate the sale, but their loyalty ultimately lies with the seller.

It is possible that an agent can represent both clients under a relationship called "Limited Disclosure Dual Agency," but this often puts them in a precarious position of trying to be fair and represent both clients, without giving up too much information or loyalty to either side. In this case both clients would be notified and asked to sign the Dual Agency disclosure form. If the seller's agent and the buyer's agent are two different people, but they both work for the same brokerage, the law considers that dual agency as well, and they will also be informed of the dual agency relationship.

There could be benefits to having the same agent for the buyer and seller. Some agents are able to be fair and represent both clients, and it would most likely make the flow of information easier and quicker between the buying and selling parties, without an extra person to go through.

But in the long run, I believe it is better to find yourself a buyer's agent to represent you and your specific needs. And the good news is that the real estate agent doesn't cost the buyer anything. The commission comes out of the seller's closing costs, so why not use this free resource?

Title and Escrow Companies

Again, I highly suggest you never buy any real estate without going through a title/escrow company. Title issues come up surprisingly frequently, often having to do with inheritance issues or divorces, and often they can be easily resolved by professionals who know how to do it. For a fairly minimal charge, it is well worth it to have the title reviewed by a reputable title company and get title insurance to protect your right to own that property. They can also tell you if there are legal easements and other issues on your land.

An escrow company is a neutral party who helps put together the deal in a legal manner and files the new purchase with the county recorder. Often, the escrow and title company are the same and will do both jobs for you.

County Assessors Office

This is one of the best places to start when researching property. This is where you can find the tax records, the assessed value of the property, permitted improvements, school districts and more, depending on your state. Most counties and states have their assessor information online now.

Surveyors

It is important to be sure that you know exactly where the boundaries of your property are. If the property has not been surveyed recently, it is worth it to hire a surveyor to find out exactly where the property lines are.

Contractors and Engineers

If you plan on building on your land, consider getting the opinion of a reliable contractor or engineer. They may be able to help you with zoning issues, material and labor costs and the permit process.

Geologists and Land Use Specialists

Consider consulting with a geologist, geotechnical engineer or land development engineer if you:

- Have any issues with land use
- Have water flow issues
- Will be doing drainage work
- Issues with soil and/or rocks
- Will be doing grading on your land
- If you will be building on a hillside
- Will be putting up retaining walls
- Will be putting in a septic system

Flood information

It's not hard to find out if your land is in a flood area. You can do this yourself by going to the FEMA flood information site to find out information on most any property in the United States. The web address is: http://www.fema.gov . Or go directly to find FEMA flood maps by entering an address, a place, or longitude/latitude coordinates here: https://msc.fema.gov/portal

Web Soil Survey Information

Most places in the US have been mapped in great detail, through many decades of soil surveys. You can find this information at the USDA Natural Resource conservation Service (NRCS) website, an online visual database used to explore the soil types within a user defined area. It shows specific soil profiles, soil types, class, depth, frequency of ponding, available water capacity, and more. Go to: http://websoilsurvey.sc.egov.usda.gov/App/HomePage.htm

Utilities

Call your local utility companies to find out if your land has any utility access.

Power company - Call to find out if electric power is supplied to the property, and if not, what it will cost to get it to the land. You may have to speak to the utility company's engineering department to get this information.

Gas and/or Propane Company – Does the local gas company supply natural gas to the land. If not, can you get propane delivered there?

Phone service - Are phone land lines available? What is the cost to get it? Can you get cell service on your land?

Sewer service – Is the property connected to a local municipal sewer service. If it can be, how much will it cost to do that?

Septic Systems— If there is no sewer system available, can you put a septic system on your land? What are the local laws and permits that will be needed. Are there any special tests that need to be done? How much will it cost to install a septic system in your area? A company that specializes in installing and inspecting septic systems should be able to answer these questions for you.

Water

Visit your state's Water Resource Department website. You might be surprised how much information you can get online. For instance, in Arizona you can get water resource information from http://www.azwater.gov/azdwr/ and for more precise information on wells, water tables, and water supply go to http://gisweb.azwater.gov/waterresourcedata/. You can also find a map of all the registered wells in Arizona at: https://gisweb.azwater.gov/WellRegistry/.

Water company - Is there a local water company in the area? Do the water lines go to the property line, and is there a meter? If not, what will it cost to get the water and meter?

Wells - If there is a well, have a well service company come out and check to be sure the well and pump are in working order. They should also be able to have the water tested to be sure it's safe for consumption. In our area there is a lot of natural arsenic in the water. It can be resolved with a special filter, but you need to know if you need one.

If there is not a well and you want to dig one, call a well digging company and find out what the well depths are in the area, as well as what the costs are to install a well.

Water Haul - In our area of Arizona, digging a well in some areas can be extremely expensive because the water levels are so deep, and the cost for a well can be $20,000 or more—often costing more than the price of the property. In this case there is usually a water delivery service available. The owners will install a tank on the property and will hire someone to deliver water or go get it themselves with a portable water tank in a truck or trailer. The cost to buy the water yourself is usually very inexpensive—pennies per gallon, depending on the area. It costs more to have it delivered, depending on how accessible your land is. This is a way of life here and in many parts of the country, where well water or municipal water is not available.

Water Collection – In some areas, rain catchment is a viable option as well. Even here in the desert, we can get some of our water from catchment. Some areas of the high desert will get enough water to take care of most of their needs, if they have a good collection system. It doesn't rain often here in the desert, but when it does, it comes down fast and hard, and if you have a big enough system to catch it, you can save it up for a while. In other areas that get more rain, like Hawaii, for instance, water catchment can be the usual method for getting your water when you are out in the country and away from city water. Check with your state to make sure this is a legal way to get your water. There are a few states, like Utah, that don't allow water collection.

Banks and Mortgage Companies

If you plan on building on your land soon, you might want to talk to your bank or mortgage company and find out about land and construction package loans. It is possible that you can put it all together in one loan, instead of waiting until after the purchase to look into the loan process.

Part 3: What to Do with Raw Land

Chapter 11

The Eleventh Secret of Wealthy Real Estate Investors: Find Uses for Your Land

So, let's say you now own some raw land, and because of the economy in the area where your land is purchased, you are unable to sell this land at this time. What can you do with it? It's just a piece of vacant land in the middle of the country or in the middle of a neighborhood.

Well, surprisingly there are quite a few options. Here are a few ideas for uses for vacant or raw land. Not all of them will apply to your situation, depending on where your land is located, but hopefully it will give you some ideas. Of course, you will need to do some research into zoning, community laws and HOA rules to be sure that what you want to do is legal and won't upset your neighbors.

Uses for Raw or Vacant Land:

1. Hang on to it. This is the most common thing land investors do. If you can afford it, just be patient, hang on to the land and wait it out. Keep paying the taxes and fees. Everything goes in cycles, so the idea is to hold the property and wait to sell your land until the economy is in a better.

2. Test it for mining. Perhaps your land has something you can use. Do you have the mineral rights? Find out if gold or other precious rocks, minerals, or gems have been discovered in your area. You could mine it yourself or lease it to some person or company that mines. Even sand, gravel and native stone can be mined and sold, or leased to someone who wants to mine it.

3. Test it for oil or gas. Find out if there may be oil, gas, natural gas or coal on your land. You could lease it to a company that drills for oil or gas production. If you live in state like Texas, Oklahoma, Arkansas, North Dakota, Alaska and California this could be a big deal.

4. Use its unique features. What are the unique advantages or features of your land? Is it on a mountain or hill top? Perhaps you can rent it out to a local astronomy club or let the local college use it for digging fossils or for unique rocks.

5. Harvest the plants on it. If the land has timber and you have the timber rights, you could consider harvesting the timber or leasing the land for logging, or even selling firewood. Perhaps it has edible or medicinal wild herbs, berry bushes or gourmet mushrooms growing on it that are in demand elsewhere. If you have maple trees, you could harvest the maple syrup or allow others to do that.

Even here in the desert we have chaparral, sage and other herbs that you could sell to people online. One woman made a good business selling tumbleweeds to people in places all over the world —for plays, decoration, and who knows what else. You might be surprised what you have growing on your land that people may want.

6. Rent it to a farmer. If you have land that is good for growing crops, consider renting it for farm or crop land. This is a popular option for many people who own land in farming areas, but it also works in some areas that may not look like farming land at first glance. Talk to the local cooperative extension or agricultural extension office and see if this is an option for you.

7. Farm something. You could grow crops yourself. There are many options besides your typical vegetables and grains. Plant an orchard or a vineyard. How about specialty herbs, gourmet mushrooms, or flowers? Sell your produce and products at a local farmers market or to local businesses.

8. Grow Landscaping Plants. Grow and sell indoor houseplants (you might need a greenhouse) or landscaping plants for nurseries. There are people here in the middle of the desert that grow and sell cactus and palm trees on their land. Some of them take time, but could give you a good return if you are patient.

9. Dig a well and sell water. Do you have water rights and a well or some other water source? I knew of a ranch near Las Vegas that sold and bottled mountain spring water from an artesian well on their property. Here in our area of the desert, there are many people out in the country who make a good living selling water from their well for pick-up, as well as hauling it to other property owners who don't have any water on their land.

10. Raise Fish. If you have a stream, pond or lake on your land, you could let fishermen come and use it for fishing or as a casting pool. You could also stock a small lake or pond and raise fish for yourself or to sell to others.

11. Grow Algae. Again, if you have a water source and some room to put in ponds, you could consider starting an algae farm. There is a big demand right now for clean organic spirulina and chlorella in health food circles.

12. Raise small or large livestock. Can you use your land to raise cattle, pigs, horses, chickens, sheep, goats, rabbits, alpacas, lamas or some kind of exotic animal? Again, do your homework and be sure this is something you can do legally and won't upset your neighbors.

13. Rent it out for pasturing animals. Lease your land out to a livestock owner who could let his livestock graze for a fee. This could work for cattle, horses, goats, alpaca, lamas, sheep and more. This is a great option if you already have fencing, a barn, electric power and/or water. If some of these things are needed and you don't have them, perhaps you could have the rancher put up their own shelters and other needed items.

14. Use it for recreation. Consider letting people who use ATV's, dirt bikes, mountain bikes, or snowmobiles come and play on your land. If you have a cabin or trailer on the property, this is even better, since you could rent it out.

15. Use it for camping. You can use the land yourself and park your trailer or RV on it, or rent it out as a place for campers, RVers, or church groups to use as a retreat. People love to go out to remote areas to camp with tents or hammocks too.

16. Build a retreat center. Put up a cabin or multiple cabins and rent it out as a spiritual retreat center.

17. Build an RV Park or Campground. If you land is suited for it and has easy access to a highway or main road, you could build an RV park or campground on it. Again, check into zoning and other laws in your community.

18. Put a petting zoo on it. Do it yourself or lease it to someone who wants to have a petting zoo there.

19. Lease it to hunters. If you have a large parcel of land that has game on it, or perhaps a lake with ducks, you could lease it to hunters to use. If you don't have any natural game, or the laws don't permit it, maybe you could raise specialty game for hunting.

20. Put up a hunting cabin. If you have a smaller lot in an area known for hunting, put up a cabin and rent it to seasonal hunters.

21. Generate electricity. Look into grants for wind turbines, solar power or other green energy. You may also be able to lease the land out to others who want to do the same thing.

22. Easement Access. If there is a landlocked property near you perhaps you could sell or lease easement access to the owners. (Or just sell them your property.) Perhaps the power or some other utility company would like easement access and you could work out a deal with them.

23. Subdivide it. Take a large parcel of land and divide it into smaller parcels you could sell separately or build on. This is another time honored strategy, but it often takes some money to do. Be sure to check with your local authorities on zoning laws, as well as fees and filing costs. You will need to get a survey as well. In some areas, like here in Arizona, you will also need to file a public report if you divide it into more than 6 lots and sell them separately, which might involve a lawyer. There may be capital gains fees too, so do your research before you start this process.

24. Develop the land. Build something. You could build a home or some other improvement to the land, such as a cabin, or even a simple storage shed. You could build anything from a spec house to a self-storage business (you will need commercial zoning) to a high rise. Then you could use it, rent it or sell the land with its improvements for a higher price.

25. Find partners. If you don't have the money to improve and build on the land, try to find a partner or partners who are willing to help develop the land with you.

26. Install a mobile home. This is a surprisingly inexpensive option compared to building a site built home.

27. Build an off-the-grid home or an underground fallout shelter. You could build it for yourself as a get-away or sell it to a "prepper" who might be interested in the same thing. If you want to go all out, stock it with food, water, and other necessities to make it an attractive property for someone to buy.

28. Lease the property to someone who wants to live off-the-grid. Let them build their off the gird home there. Someone might be interested in having an off-the-grid home, but can't afford the land or maybe doesn't want their name on it as a property owner.

29. Build a tree house. Have lots of trees on your land? Tree houses are popular right now and you could easily rent it out if you wanted to.

30. Build an eco-friendly green home. Green homes such as earth bermed (halfway underground) are popular energy saving eco-friendly alternatives that many people are looking for. Similar types of homes are also rammed earth, hay bale homes, true adobe homes, and Earthships.

31. Use the property for storage. Use it yourself for storage or rent it to others. Land that is conveniently located and has a barn, fencing or storage containers on it can be used for storage for construction machinery, landscape supplies, boats, snowmobiles, ATV's, etc.

32. Put a "tiny home" on it. Tiny homes are very popular currently as low-impact and low-cost housing. You can build one for yourself, rent it out, or build one to help sell the property. There are

many varieties of tiny homes, from tree houses to yurts. One low-cost option that is popular here is to make a cargo container into a small house or cabin. For more information on low cost cargo container homes go to: www.custom-container-homes.com
(*Disclaimer – the author has some interest in this particular company and may make some profit from sales and referrals.)

33. Sell things. If your land is in a high traffic area where people can access it easily, consider selling stuff from it. Some ideas: vehicles, firewood, landscaping plants or trees.

34. Hold events. How about having a concert or festival on your land; or host a seasonal farmers market or flee market. Let non-profit organization have their rummage sales or school carnivals on it.

35. Educate people. Use your land to teach others how to live off the land.

36. Outdoor photography. If your land has great scenery and view, bring tour groups to take pictures.

37. Establish a Scenic Overlook. If you have good access to busy traffic as well as great views, consider establishing a scenic overlook.

38. Make it into a Paintball Field. Charge people money to come out and use it for paintball. Or lease it out to a paintball club.

39. Turn it into an outdoor obstacle course. Charge people money to run through it. If your land is on a slope, put up a zip line for people to use.

40. Make an outdoor shooting range. Turn your land into a place where people can go to practice shooting their guns, or use it for archery or paintball.

41. Make a boat launch. If you have access to water, let people use your land as a boat launch.

42. Form an HOA. If you find yourself owning worthless land or land where the developer disappeared or has filed bankruptcy and there are no utilities or even road access or maintenance, you might consider writing to the other owners of the development and forming a Home Owners Association. A minimal yearly fee can do wonders for getting roads plowed, bringing in electrical power or even drilling a well for the community to access.

43. Donate your land. Find a non-profit organization that could use the money and/or the land. This is a good option if you are philanthropically inclined and/or you want to get the tax savings.

44. Turn it into a community park, garden, dog park or playground. Again for those who are altruistically inclined, you could do something with your land that will better the community.

45. Preserve wildlife. If you have a large parcel and a lot of natural wildlife, or have wetlands, you could turn your land into a wildlife preserve.

46. Use it for outdoor trails. Pave a bike or walking path on your land. If you have a lot of land, consider making hiking, quad and off-road vehicles, cross-country skiing or snowmobile trails.

47. Make an athletic field. Perhaps your land would be just right for a soccer, baseball or football field.

48. Sell outdoor advertising. If our land is near a road and in a high traffic area, you could put up a billboard or lease your land to a sign company. Be sure you check on zoning and permits.

49. Sell parking. This is a good option if you have a busy business near your land, such as a truck stop, restaurant, flea market, or a hotel that needs extra overnight parking.

50. Cell towers. Consider leasing your property for cell tower use.

51. Make a Landfill. If you have a large property, you could consider making it into a landfill. Trash has to go somewhere. Of course you need to check into getting all the proper licenses, permits, etc.

52. Build a golf course. Perhaps you can turn your property into a golf course. How about a miniature golf course or a driving range?

53. Make a drive-in movie theater. This can be a popular novelty these days.

54. Build a Track. Put a racetrack on your land. There are all types of things that need racetracks such as: cars, horses, slot cars and bumper cars, greyhounds, BMX bikes, skateboards, radio control vehicles, etc.

These are just a few ideas to get you thinking. Be creative and think outside the box. There are many ways you can put your land to good use and turn it into an asset. Just be sure to do the proper research and due diligence before you get started on your project. It is surprising what a person can do with a simple plot of dirt that everyone else ignored.

Chapter 12

The Twelfth Secret of Wealthy Real Estate Investors: Know How to Sell Your Land

Selling land is different than selling a home and has its own unique challenges. I have already talked about knowing when to sell your land. The best time is when everyone is buying land in your area. In this case, if your land is priced right, and located in a good area, there should be no problem selling.

Unfortunately, this is usually not the case for most land sellers. Land sales are usually not as active as home sales markets. Sellers can't always control the timing for their need to sell. They may have inherited a piece of property and need to get the cash from it. Some sellers end up with sudden medical debts that necessitate the sale of the property to help pay for them. Perhaps they just decided that they don't have a use for the land they bought. Whatever the reason, land sellers need to know how to sell their property, like the wealthy real estate investors do, even in a sluggish market. Even if you have a real estate agent helping you sell, there are still things you can take action and do, to help get your land sold faster and reach that group of land investment buyers.

The first step is to know your market.

How active is it? Is it a buyer's market or a seller's market? A buyer's market is one where the buyers can pretty much pick their prices. A seller's market is one where the sellers drive the prices. A balanced market is one that is just like it sounds. Both the buyers and the sellers determine the price points.

Are properties selling in your area right now? Has there been any new development in the area? Have they added any utilities or other amenities?

Once you know your market, it will be easier to decide on a price to offer your property at.

Know your buyers - land buyers are different than home buyers

Do they want to build a home or homes or do they want to buy as in investment or for recreation purposes - focus your message for your targeted buyers.

Price it right

This is very important— one of the biggest mistakes sellers make is pricing their property too high. One way to avoid this is to compare your property to others on the market.

When looking at comparables, there are a few things to keep in mind:

- Try to find properties that are close to the same size as yours. Often larger parcels are discounted more by price per acre. It is better to find properties as close to the size of yours as you can.
- You also want to find properties that are as close to the location of your land as possible. Sometimes land in the same subdivision, but in a different unit or area of it, can be very different in price. In our area, some units have utilities and some don't, directly affecting the price.
- Access is important too. Do the properties you are comparing yours to have similar access?
- Try to find several properties for sale and several properties that have sold, so you can see the difference between the sale price and listing price. This should help you determine what your land is worth on the market. Remember, it is not

what you paid for (or even what the tax price says) that determines what a property is worth, but rather what the market will give you at the time of the sale.
- How fast do you want to sell? You may have to choose between selling fast and getting a good price if you are in a hurry. Any property can sell fast in just about any market, if the price is low enough.

Other factors that are involved in pricing include:

- Does the property have any improvements that can add value to the land? Things such as wells, storage containers, barns and sheds, septic systems, fencing, etc. can add help you get a better price for your land.
- Is the property on or near water? Land that has water frontage usually is worth more.
- Does the property have utilities to the property line? How far away are the utilities, if it does not?

Look at your land from a buyer's point of view.

Who would your potential buyer be? What do they want to know about your land?

Take some great pictures and use lots of them. Show the area, the roads, the neighborhood, the views, the boundaries of the lot, and area attractions.

Marketing

Again, a good agent can help you with this process, but you can also do things to help market and sell the property yourself, and help your often very busy agent out and help get your land sold faster.

Remember, most real estate contracts include the stipulation that the agent gets paid their commission, even if you sell the property yourself. The reason for this is that each listing costs the listing agent at least $100 or more—for signs, travel for photographs and to check out the property, administrative help, doing research on property (including zoning, flood areas, ownership, maps, …) and lots of time spent marketing, doing paperwork and talking to potential buyers.

But, even if you have an agent helping you sell, you can do things that will help sell and market the property as well.

Offer seller financing.

It is very difficult to get bank loans on land. Seller financing will give you larger pool of potential buyers. Plus you can get more money over the long run by charging interest. So if you don't need to sell immediately, this is a great way to sell your property, especially in a slow market.

Typical owner carry deals for land would be 15 – 30% down. Remember you need to get enough money to cover the closing costs and real estate agents' commissions, as well as some you can hopefully pocket. The length of the loan time varies, depending on how long you are willing to carry the loan. I see loan periods that go from 2 years to 20. Typically it is 5-10 years. Owner carry interest rates are typically a little higher than the commercial market interest rates. Of course, these are all negotiable issues.

Have your land ready to view.

What your land looks like often does make a difference. Does it need to be cleaned up? If you can, cut the grass and/or weeds. Get rid of any trash, wood piles and excess items littering the property.

Some people even scatter wildflower seeds to make the property more appealing. Some properties can even be staged with outdoor furniture, a fire pit, etc.

Consider having a survey done and mark the property boundaries.

It makes a big difference in selling a property if potential buyers can see exactly where the boundaries of the land are. Many buyers like to walk the land and find those markers. If you have an official survey done, you can also show them the map. It saves the buyer from having to do the survey themselves. It makes your property more marketable since many other competing properties for sale will not have a recent survey.

Put Up a Sign.

Make sure there is a "for sale" sign on the property. This alerts locals and neighbors, as well as people who drive by looking for land for sale. It also helps people locate your land if they found it on the internet and are doing their due diligence.

Make a web page for your land.

Have a webpage and/or a Facebook business page. Send the link to everyone in your network. Perhaps they know someone who is looking for land. Include the real estate agent's contact info, if you have one. (Please let the agent know you are doing this, though, to make sure it works with the agent's marketing. Usually agents don't have any problem with it, since it helps them, too.)

Write down everything you can think of that will describe your property, including a written description and lots of photographs, perhaps taken in different seasons, information about the local area, last year's real estate taxes, aerial photos, road maps and a PDF or JPG copy of the survey, if available. If you have a Realtor®, give this information to them. It will help them tools to improve the marketing of your property.

Use online and print classified ads.

Again, if you have an agent, check with them to be sure this will work with their marketing efforts. They may appreciate the help, or it may get in their way if they are already doing the same. You could offer to pay for print advertising or specialized listings that will highlight your property on websites such as Landwatch.com or LandandFarm.com.

Talk to the neighbors. Talking to the neighbors in the area, as well as the home owners association is a good idea. Let them know your land is for sale. Perhaps they would be interested in picking out their new neighbors, or perhaps they would like to add to the land they already own in the area.

Send Letters to Neighbors. Send out letters to the surrounding property owners if you are unable to talk in person to them. You may be able to get the addresses from the county accessor's office or from a title company, or ask your real estate agent if they can supply the address for you.

Connect with some of the other sellers in your area.

Perhaps you can work together to share buyer leads or advertise your land together. Find out what they are doing to market their property. Share ideas.

Also contact active builders in the area to let them know you are selling. Your land might be just what they were looking for.

Put up flyers around town and on community bulletin boards. Look for community bulletin boards near the property or just put them up on bulletin and ad boards wherever you live. The more you get the word out, the better chance you will have to sell your property

Create a short video showcasing your property and post it on YouTube. Some people are more visual and get a better feel for the property by seeing a video of it. A video that has been done well can give your property an advantage over other similar properties for sale. Consider hiring a professional videographer to do this for you.

Another good reason to do a video is that videos get better online rankings for searches than websites do.

Auction Websites such as eBay I've seen some owners sell their land quickly on eBay and other online auction sites. Also you can put property listings up on eBay as well, just for the advertising. You don't actually sell it though the auction process. Remember, though, that people who go to auction sites are looking for a good deal and usually want to pay less than they would through traditional methods.

Connect with Investors. Use the Biggerpockets Marketplace (www.Biggerpockets.com), Facebook, Linkedin and other places to connect with investors online.

Be patient. As I mentioned before, land is not a fluid investment and it often takes longer to sell land than a home. If the market isn't right for selling at the moment, wait a bit and it will change.

Work with Professionals. Listing your property with a professional real estate broker who specializes and understands land sales is always helpful. They can help you understand the market, set a price and market your land to the right buyers.

Although this is not the right choice for everyone, there are advantages in listing with a real estate agent:

You don't have to deal with calls from people who are "looky-loos" and people who are just curious, like neighbors.

By using professionals, your property should be marketed better and have a greater target market reach. First, it will be included in the MLS, which is sent out to Zillow, Trulia, and other top websites. In my case, our brokerage sends out the listing information to over 400 websites, including some international sites. As I mentioned earlier, most real estate sales today are searched for on the internet. You want to make sure that your property can be easily found there.

If your real estate agent works a lot with land, they may know of investors and others in their network that are looking for land in the area.

A good agent who sells land will be able to help you with the selling process and issues concerning zoning, state laws, etc.

Conclusion

Now that you have read through this book, it is time to put some thought into what direction you want to go with your land investment. Go to the appendix at the back of this book and find the worksheet to help you build your land business plan. Don't skip this step. Think about land ownership like a business.

Land investment, like any investment, can be risky. Even if you do all your due diligence and research, things can still happen. There are natural disasters like wildfires, floods or earthquakes. There are economic disasters that can deflate the price of land. Some things just can't be predicted, but with enough investigative research, you can certainly cut many of the risk factors down.

The main thing to look for when buying land as an investment is that you want to buy land that is in the path of growth. You want usable land, for whatever purpose you want to use it for. Usually, this includes good access and utilities.

Keep an eye out for bargains when buying land. They can be found in any market if you search hard enough. Get to know the prices and everything you can find out about the area you want to buy in.

On the other hand, owning land can be incredibly rewarding. With land, you have a tangible asset that you can use for building, farming, recreation, hunting, development or for some other purpose like making a wildlife refuge.

With the economy the way it is right now, many people are concerned that interest rates will skyrocket and perhaps there will even be hyperinflation in the United States. Traditionally real estate has been a good investment hedge in times like this. Countless people have bought land at the right time in the right place and sold it at the right time to make huge profits. They did their research and followed their instincts, and this is one of the major secrets of the wealthy real estate investors.

Whether you're just starting the process of investing your land, or you have been doing it for many years, I hope this book has helped you.

Thanks and good luck with your real estate land investments!

Appendix A

Land Business Plan

Fill in the following questions below to build your plan:

1. 1. Why do I plan on investing in land? What do I want to accomplish?

    Do I want to buy and hold?

    Will I be building a retirement or an inheritance for my children?

    Do I want to wait until the prices go up and sell?

    Do I want to quickly flip land?

    Do I want land to diversify my investments?

    Do I want to build a home on this land?

    Do I want the land for recreation purposes?

    Do I want to farm or ranch on my land?

2. How do I plan on paying for the land?

    Do I have a budget for this?

    Do I have cash (or something else) for a down payment?

    Will I be financing the land, and if so, with a bank or with the owner?

3. How am I going to find the land I want to buy?

4. How will I do my "due diligence"?

5. Do I mind having an HOA?

Appendix B

Due Diligence List

1. Get Price Comparisons of Similar Properties

2. Physical Land Use Due Diligence

    a. Locate the boundaries and find or do any surveys need.

    b. Find Aerial maps and topographical maps.

    b. View the slope and elevation of the land.

    c. Check the vegetation.

    d. Determine the water flow and washes.

    e. Determine who has the mineral and water rights.

    e. Research environmental reports and issues:

       Protected areas like wetland delineation.

       Protected/endangered animal species studies.

    f. Geotechnical and soils reports and perc tests.

3. Legal, Development and Regulatory Issues

    a. Zoning verification.

    b. City and County Ordinances.

    c. Land development regulations.

    c. Building regulations.

d. Permitted and conditional uses.

d. Cultural resources/historical survey.

e. Tax information.

f. Restrictions - land use, location of home, manufactured home, RV parking, etc.

g. Determine the approval and permitting process

4. Improvements

    a. Learn the access to utilities and utility verification

    b. Get the water and/or sewer maps, if possible.

    b. Fencing.

    c. Sheds and outbuildings— Make sure you get in writing what is going to stay and what you want removed.

    d. Wells and water storage tanks.

    e. Septic systems.

    f. RV hookups.

    g. Any other improvements.

5. Access and Roads

    a. Determine the road access, offsite road improvements & onsite road circulation.

    b. Try to find out about any future road information.

    c. Road maintenance.

6. Title Issues

    a. Correct ownership.

    b. Liens and financial issues.

    c. Any easements, dedications and encroachments.

    d. Title policy with copies of all exceptions.

7. Get any pertinent information about the POA or HOA.

Sources:

http://www.realtor.org/sites/default/files/Study-Digital-House-Hunt-2013-01_1.pdf

https://en.wikipedia.org/wiki/Multiple_listing_service

https://en.wikipedia.org/wiki/Geographic_information_system

https://en.wikipedia.org/wiki/Homeowner_association

https://en.wikipedia.org/wiki/Planned_unit_development

http://www.investopedia.com/terms/d/duediligence.asp

http://www.investopedia.com/terms/h/hoa.asp

###END##

www.ingramcontent.com/pod-product-compliance
Lightning Source LLC
Chambersburg PA
CBHW062115220526
45471CB00010B/3745